5 secrets

for peace in a storm

**A fresh dose
of unstoppable
courage**

by
Ruthie Jacobsen

5 Secrets for Peace in a Storm

Cover and interior design, Bryan Gray

Cover photo copyright © Darren Baker

Published by HighWalk Productions Inc.

P O Box 26, Hiawassee, GA 30546

ISBN 978-0-615-23305-5

PRINTED IN U.S.A.

Go to www.5SecretsForPeaceInaStorm.com for further information and also for
other inspirational products.

Table of Contents

DEDICATION

This book is dedicated to you,

Wendy Matheison Andrew

Wendy (right) celebrates with her sister Molly, after completing the Trek Woman's Triathlon Series Event in September 2009, her third.

You are the epitome of an unstoppable
and courageous young woman.
All of us who know you have learned
much as we have watched you navigate
your own storm and still radiate peace.

Wendy was diagnosed with breast cancer early in 2008. After surgery she faced extended chemotherapy treatments followed by radiation, additional surgery, and still more chemotherapy.

But Wendy's spirit gives new meaning to the word unstoppable. She determined that because her faith in God would provide all the strength she needed, life would go on and her passion for helping others would never abate.

During the numerous medical procedures, she never missed a day of work except for those days on which she was actually scheduled for treatments.

Through it all Wendy finished two mini-triathlons, biked, hiked, swam, jogged, and as this is being written, another mini-triathlon is on her calendar. In the worst of her own stress she demonstrated her unflagging sense of humor when she bought T-shirts for all of her extended family that said, "Suck it up, Cupcake."

Wendy's secret is her indomitable faith in her God, her remarkable sense of humor, and her willingness to keep constantly searching for ways to bless others.

Wendy, we love you. We're proud of you. You're a classic example of the message of this book.

Introduction

We're living in some pretty tough times...you've noticed that, I'd guess. I'll bet you've said, as I have, "Wow, I've never seen anything like this before in my lifetime."

Look around...the economy, unemployment, health issues, drugs, the divorce rate, foreclosures, crime...you don't need to be reminded. It takes courage just to watch the news anymore.

And it seems we've become a nation riddled with new permissibles: abortion, porn, drugs, divorce, the Internet; the very moral fiber of our nation is being challenged.

It affects our schools, our families, our corporations, even our churches. We're all touched in some degree by what's going on around us.

That's why I hope you'll read this book. It is full of public secrets of things we can do to change how we are affected by our world. I've decided I'm not going to just whine about what's going on but rather do something about it. You'll find some very practical suggestions here.

We learn much from storms. Storms are growing times,

stretching times, maturing times. They broaden us, even as they frighten us.

They teach us even as they confront us. But we choose whether we are going to be engulfed by them and sink, or engage them and come away stronger.

One more thing, this is not a book about nice theories, it's not about something I read somewhere. It is in many ways a description of my own journey. I've discovered how storms change me and bless me and make me strong and make me sensitive to the storms of others. So this will be our journey together.

Come, let's get started.

Chapter 1

What Did You Say?

As I ponder the power of the word to incite and divide, to calm and connect, or to create and effect change, I am ever more cautious in what I say and how I listen to the words around me.
—Susan Smalley

The last thing you said changed who you are.

Others may have heard it, too, but it changed *you* more than it did *them*. When your mouth talks, your ears listen. No matter what anyone else says about you, what you say about you has a greater affect on you.

My husband tells about a distant auntie in his family whose theme in life seemed to be, "Ain't it awful." It didn't matter the situation or the story or the circumstances, her stock reply was, "Ain't it awful?" You've probably met people like that, too. But if we say it often enough we can begin to believe it. We can even begin to develop an "Ain't it awful?" mindset.

Let me tell you a story. I know, even with the best of pedigrees, stories that circulate on the Internet are often difficult to validate. This one I recently read may be true or not. If you have a question about that, just consider it a parable. Its profound insight is too valuable to miss.

"Last week, I took my children to a restaurant. My six-year-old son asked if he could say grace. As we bowed our heads he said, 'God is good, God is great. Thank You for the food, and I would even thank You more if Mom gets us ice cream for dessert. And liberty and justice for all! AMEN.'

"Along with the quiet chuckles from some of the other customers nearby, I heard a woman remark, 'That's what's wrong with our country...kids today don't even know how to pray. Asking God for ice cream! Why, I never!'

"Hearing this, my son got big tears in his eyes and asked me, 'Mom, is God mad at me?' As I assured him that he had done a terrific job, an elderly gentleman approached our table. He said, 'I happen to know that God thought that was a great prayer.'

"'Really?' my son asked.

"'Cross my heart,' the man replied. Then in a whisper, he added (indicating the woman whose remark had started the whole thing), 'Too bad she never asks God for ice cream. A little ice cream is good for the soul sometimes.'

"Naturally, I bought my kids ice cream at the end of the meal. My son stared at his for a moment, and then did something I will remember the rest of my life. He picked up his sundae and, without a word, walked over and placed it in front of the woman. With a big smile he told her, 'Here, this is for you. Ice cream is good for the soul sometimes; and my soul is good already!'"

"Mom, is God mad at me?" It's not hard to see how a six-year old might ask that question, and a lot of adults do, too. But it's wonderful to see in the story the wisdom of the mother and the kindness of the man in planting healthy new seeds in the little boy's mind.

The New Testament tells the story of Jesus' disciples rowing across the Sea of Galilee late one night when a storm arose. The storm was severe enough that the disciples, most of whom were seasoned sailors, were terrified. Their frantic appeal was, "Master, don't You care that we're all going to drown?" Jesus replied in effect, "Don't doubt; just trust."

In times of difficulty, God is honored and our hearts are encouraged when we speak words of confidence and positive trust. When you faced your last storm, What did you say? Did you tell God how big your storm was or did you tell the storm how big your God is?

The same principle shows up in the Old Testament.

Just seventy-two hours before David was to be proclaimed king over all of Israel, he went through one of the deepest, darkest valleys of his life. He and his band of ragtag soldiers had been out patrolling the borders of Israel and, returning home they saw smoke rising from the direction of their own village.

They must have run, armor clanking, to investigate because this was their home. Imagine their shock to discover that everything they held dear was gone—their wives, their

The *last thing*
you said
changed who
you *are.*

children, and everything they owned.

The Bible says, "They wept until they could weep no more." (The story is recorded in I Samuel 30.)

Then, just when it seemed things could get no worse for David, his men turned on him, blaming him for their loss, and threatened to stone him.

At this point a profound insight shows up in the story. Just when David has nowhere to turn, and there is no help in sight, the Bible says that David "encouraged himself in the Lord." Instead of rehearsing the frightening extremities of the situation, he agreed with God's word. David's ears heard his mouth speak words of hope.

As David remembered God's promises and His goodness in the past he felt his strength returning. Before long he could say to his men, "Come, we're going to find those thugs and recover everything we've lost!" (My paraphrase.)

His strong words of faith stirred something good and powerful in their hearts as well. He *spoke* his faith, and it not only breathed courage into his own heart, it energized his dispirited troops. Within hours, everything they had lost was recovered.

Strong Scripture principle: We actually give life to our faith *by our words*. Our faith is voice-activated.

An interesting phenomenon about the human brain is that our own words influence our minds more than anything anyone else may say. Your mind takes your tongue very seriously.

So, are you in a storm? See one approaching? Fearing one might arise? Make sure your ears hear your tongue breathe hope and trust and confidence in the God who knows how to manage storms. God wants you to believe, to hope, to expect, and to thank Him, even before you see the evidence of His wonderful answers.

No wonder the prophet Joel urges, "Let the weak **say** I am strong."

No wonder King Solomon, the wisest and richest man who ever lived could say, "Life and death are in the tongue."

Agree with God. He says He gives strength to the weak. God wants you to speak words of faith and courage about your situation. Rather than using your words to describe your situation—how it looks from a merely human perspective— agree with God's word. What did you say? I'll bet it was words of faith and hope and confidence. That's how you agree with God.

Our words can be used to change others' lives, too. Another story...

From Korea, a pastor tells the story of a distraught mother who came to him for counsel. As she described her situation, the discouragement and grief were evident in her face and her voice.

"Our lovely daughter," she moaned, "has become a prostitute. We've tried everything we can think of to help her see what she is doing to herself—to her future—and to our family. We've tried money, pleading, tears, kindness, prayer, counsel, but she's getting worse. My husband and son are very ashamed and we're all at the end of our rope. I've almost decided that if she should end her life it might be better, because she is so unhappy, on such a destructive, downward path."

"How are you praying for your daughter?" the pastor asked.

"I plead with God to change her," the mother replied.

"I want you to do something different," the pastor responded. "Let's kneel here in this office right now, and I just want you to thank God for giving you such a beautiful daughter. Thank Him for all the joy she has brought to your family as she was growing up. Just thank Him for blessing your family through this girl."

So they knelt and, struggling at first, the mother finally was able to pray a prayer that was positive, and filled with gratitude. She felt some of the burden lift after placing it in God's hands with thankful words.

"Now, remember, as you pray for your daughter every day," the pastor reminded, "pray just like that. Just thank God for your beautiful daughter and thank Him that He is working in her life. He loves her too. Jesus died to save her."

The mother returned home and as difficult as it was, kept disciplined in her thoughts and words. She read Scripture promises that encouraged her faith. Often through the day she prayed, thanking God for her sweet, beautiful daughter, her princess.

One morning, some weeks after the mother's visit with her pastor, the girl awoke lying in bed beside someone she had never seen before. She couldn't remember the evening that led up to this situation, and she was horrified at what she had become. Her thoughts were filled with remorse, guilt, and loathing. The only escape she could think of was to "end it all."

But the thought kept coming to her that before committing suicide she should go home and say good-bye to her family. So she dressed, took a cab to their home, and walked up the sidewalk to the front door.

Her mother saw her coming, and running to embrace her girl, her first words were, "Here is my beautiful daughter; the one who has brought us so much joy. I'm overjoyed to see you!"

The daughter couldn't believe her ears. She didn't feel beautiful, or joyful. She felt undeserving of her mother's love, but her mother would hear nothing of it and stopped her mid-sentence.

She brought her into the house, fixed her a nice breakfast, and then taking her to her room, she opened the bed and told her just to rest a while. The girl discovered that she was suddenly surrounded by faith-filled words of kindness and love. Slowly she began to see herself as loved and valued. Soon she was able to reach out to the God who was working to soften and change her heart.

She began to attend church again with her family, gave her heart to Christ and God completely changed her. In time she met and married a wonderful young Christian man, and for the past twenty years they have lived fulfilled and happy lives and reared two beautiful, healthy teens. Our words have the power to bring discouragement and withering hurt to others. But they also can give life, hope, and healing.

So, What did you say?

I'll bet it was words of life-giving hope, affirmation, and courage.

If you remember the early stories from the Bible record you will recall the time when Moses was mentoring Joshua, the one who was to be his successor to lead the Israelites on the last leg of their journey into the Promised Land.

Moses reminds Joshua of all God has done...the miracles in the desert to relieve their hunger and thirst...miracles in warfare over their enemies. Then he gives him a solemn warning: *"As you ponder the obstacles yet to be overcome, don't look around and tell yourself, 'We can't do this.'* Remember what He has done in the past. He will do it again. There is no need to be afraid."

Moses is giving Joshua a very important lesson in faith and leadership. He says, *"Don't tell yourself you can't,* watch your words; your own faith will be weakened or strengthened by what you say, and your people will be influenced by what you say as well." Moses understood that what we tell ourselves has momentous meaning.

During what was perhaps the most dangerous period of the Second World War the death-defying words of Sir Winston Churchill brought hope and courage when both were scarce in England. On May 13, 1940, Churchill said, "I have nothing to offer but blood, toil, tears, and sweat... You ask, what is our aim? I can answer in one word. It is victory...victory, however long and hard the road may be..."

Later Churchill would say, "We shall fight on the beaches... we shall fight on the streets..." and then he closed by saying,

"...This is [our] finest hour." These words from the Prime Minister of England still stir people everywhere with new resolve to keep trying. Many historians believe that Churchill's hope-filled words changed the morale of a nation and the course of history.

So, What did you say? What did you say when the way was tough? When the critics were loud? When your dreams didn't move the way you had hoped? When a huge loss came? When someone handed you a shattering disappointment?

I know the answer to those questions. Your words spoke courage to your own heart as you claimed the promises of God. Your tongue spoke hope to those around you. You chose to claim the promises of God and rest secure in the knowledge of His love for you.

When your mouth spoke, it breathed courage into your own heart and encouragement into those around you.

Your mind
takes your tongue
very seriously.

Chapter 2

Your Thankful List

"Gratitude unlocks the fullness of life... Gratitude makes sense of our past, brings peace for today, and creates a vision for tomorrow."
—Melody Beattie

I t took a ten-year old to challenge and humble me," says Rafe Esquith, a teacher in the inner-city of Los Angeles. It was the first day of a new school year. The trouble-makers from the year before were gone, but he says, "My nerves were exposed and raw." He didn't feel that he was in "the right mood" to be a good teacher, he just knew that no kid was going to "...use and abuse me like those ingrates from the year before had done. It was easier to be mad at them than to be mad at myself," he recalls.

As the students entered the classroom that first day, a tiny little girl with bangs came up to him. In a bag she had some breakfast food purchased at a fast-food store, and she told him that she had bought him breakfast for their first day together.

"What's your name?" I asked her.

"'Joann,' she said quietly.

"'Well, listen then, Joann,' I told her, 'You don't have to buy me breakfast or kiss up to me. If you want to be successful in this class, just do your best and we'll get along just fine—but no presents—got it?'

"'Yes,' she said meekly, and found a seat.

"'The first week went by smoothly. On Friday I gathered the students in what they call a Magic Circle. The students sit in a circle and share their feelings about any and all issues, ranging from school subjects to family problems.'

"'Well,' I told them proudly, 'I think we've had a good first week. Our reading and math have been excellent, and everyone is doing a fine job.

"'Does anyone have anything to say about this week we've spent together?'

"For the first time since Monday, Joann raised her hand. 'I have something to say,' she began. 'You know, last Monday, when I brought you breakfast, I wasn't trying to kiss up to you. You really don't understand.' She went on softly but with the determination and confidence of someone speaking the truth from the heart.

"'I've been waiting my whole life to be in your class. Ever since I was a first-grader, I've watched your class. You always have the coolest things. You have the best kids. You have great plays and play the best music. Your kids have the most fun. My parents think you're a god. They've seen you on television and read about you in newspapers and magazines.' (Rafe had received the Disney National Outstanding Teacher of the Year award.).

"Man, the room was quiet. This little girl was on a roll.

"'I wasn't trying to kiss up to you. I was just so happy to be here that I wanted to tell you that. I wanted to tell you how happy I was that I was going to have you for my teacher. And you really hurt my feelings.'"

Here was a little girl whose only desire was to say 'thank you,' and she had been misunderstood. Yet her gratitude was so genuine and so real that nothing, not even the curt comments of her fourth-grade teacher, could dampen it.

Rafe, the teacher, goes on to say, "I was devastated. This little girl spoke so simply and honestly that there was only one thing I could do. I apologized to Joann that day, and promised her that if she ever gave me another chance, I would never treat her like that again."

Rafe Esquith, in his fascinating book, "There Are No Shortcuts,"* tells how his life was profoundly impacted that day by a little girl with a grateful heart. Gratitude can do that. Joann was choosing to be grateful for her abundance, and her little 10-year old heart grew larger through the choice.

Gratitude is always a choice. It is a decision to focus on and to be grateful for what we have, rather than to focus on our losses.

Several years ago I heard Dr. Robert Schuller, pastor of the Crystal Cathedral in southern California, tell an amazing story from his own family. Dr. Schuller and his wife, Arvella, were

*Cited from, "There Are No Shortcuts," copyright 2003 by Rafe Esquith, published by Anchor Books, a Division of Random House Inc, New York. Used by permission.

traveling in Korea when they received an urgent phone call from home. Their teenage daughter, Carol, had been involved in a serious motorcycle accident and it appeared that she might lose one of her legs.

In anguish they rushed home and to their daughter's hospital room. What would you have said as you stood at that bedside under similar circumstances?

As their senses took it all in and they saw the stump of her leg elevated and swathed in bandages with the slight stain of blood showing through, they were devastated.

They fumbled for words but Carol spoke first. She said, "Dad, I've been lying here thinking about all the people who have lost arms and legs, all the people who have had bad things happen to them... You know, there is a lot of ministry to be done among those people, and that is what I am going to do."

We might have understood if she had fallen into self-pity. She could have become resentful, bitter, angry at life. Many in her situation have done just that. But instead, she chose to look beyond her loss and be thankful for the new doors of service it would open for her.

She trusted that God could use her. She assumed that her life had purpose, a purpose that even disappointment and pain could not destroy. Such is the power of gratitude.

Gratitude makes us more optimistic. It helps us think more creatively. A thankful heart makes us more alert and interested. It brings happiness and makes us more likable. People who are thankful tend to bounce back from adversity and difficulty.

I like the attitude of Vivian Greene who said, "Life is not

about waiting for the storms to pass...it's about learning to dance in the rain."

Thanksgiving can have powerful rewards for both the giver and receiver.

Gratitude enlarges our vision and focuses it on the future, giving it deeper meaning. And remember, it is generally not in serene times we grow, but rather in our storms.

But how do we develop a thankful heart in a time of crisis? How can we be sincerely thankful *in a storm?* It may often be difficult to see reasons to be grateful when the wind is still blowing, but gratitude is not based on feelings. We *choose* to be grateful. We *choose* to find reasons to be thankful—to remember to count our blessings.

In Scripture, the apostle Paul makes a rather startling statement when he tells us to *be thankful in all things.* That's in every situation, whether we get what we want or not...be thankful anyway. Find something, some reason to look up and express thanks. That is not to suggest that we are to be thankful *for* everything, but *in every situation.*

There is an amazing Old Testament story involving King David. When the king was facing a difficult battle he gathered his troops together to praise the Lord and to *thank God* for the victory—*before the battle even began.* (Ps. 20 is the song he taught them.) David knew that God was trustworthy, that He had promised to fight his battles, as He has ours. So no matter how things look in our circumstances...to your human eyesight...we can always give thanks. God is still on His throne, and He has promised that *all* things will work together for

good to those who love Him. (Romans 8:28.) That is indeed reason to be thankful!

Pastor Glenn Coon tells of a visit he made to see a woman who, he had been told, was terribly depressed. She hadn't been out of her house for weeks. The blinds in her house were shut tight. She didn't answer the door bell. She often stayed in bed all day.

When Pastor Coon and his wife went to visit the woman, they were surprised at what they saw...a thin, unhappy woman, hair uncombed, dressed in pajamas, robe and slippers. Her drooping shoulders and furrowed brow told the story.

Reluctantly the woman invited them in, and when Pastor

It is not in serene times we grow, but rather in our storms.

Coon asked how she was feeling, she launched into a long negative recital of her unhappy life.

But Pastor Coon soon stopped her. In his visitation, he had learned that it was not helpful for the person to wallow in a long description of the problems. Rather, he would spend a few minutes listening to the tale of woe, but then he would skillfully steer the conversation toward the solution.

So he tactfully stopped her, and said, "Now I know things have been difficult, but let's think of some ways we can change this situation." She replied with a skeptical look.

Pastor Coon told her about the beauty and power of a thankful heart. "What do you have to be thankful for?" he asked this woman who was surrounding herself with an environment of darkness. She seldom turned the lights on...never let the sunshine in.

"I have *nothing* to be thankful for," she insisted.

"Well, can you *see*?" he asked her. "Do you have good vision? Can you read good books, can you see the birds and squirrels outside?"

He continued, "Can you hear music, the voices of friends and loved ones? Can you hear a plane flying overhead, the sounds of children playing?" She assured him she had the use of all of those senses. "God has given you the wonderful gifts of vision, hearing, taste, touch, and smell. That's a good place to start."

Then he told her he'd like for her to do something specific that would take some deliberate decisions, but he promised her it was worth it. He asked her to make a written list of ten things for which she was thankful, and to add the names of family members and friends she loved and who loved her.

What he told her next shocked her. He said, "I want you to thank God once every hour for each of these items on your 'thankful list.' Every hour that you are awake I want you to repeat this process. Thank Him for at least ten things every hour. Look outside. Thank Him for the trees, the green grass, flowers, sunshine, rain. Ask Him to give you a thankful heart."

She thought about it for a long time. At first she resisted. It seemed foolish to be thanking God when she didn't *feel* thankful. But Pastor Coon understood that *often feelings follow actions.*

They prayed together and asked God to give her special strength and resolve to carry out the plan. She finally agreed to "give it a try," even though it seemed ludicrous to her at the time.

In a matter a weeks there was a marked difference. When he went back to see her, the blinds were up, sunlight was streaming into the house, she had obviously showered and shampooed her hair; she was dressed in a colorful housedress, and had even done some housework.

She began caring for her garden. She had found new hope and was finding healing. Why? She was choosing to focus on another picture—the reality of God's love and care. She was thanking Him for specific things, and choosing to find reasons to be grateful.

Being grateful to God is essential because thanksgiving is the expression of thanks to God for something specific He has done just for you.

He wants us to be specific, because He is specific in His blessings. He wants us to notice His faithfulness. He loves to have us remember specific times when He has done something special. And if we try to list them, they are too numerous to count.

No wonder King David reminds us again and again to praise the Lord, and to sing to Him our gratitude and worship. Sometimes singing is a neglected part of our personal worship and devotion time. But our gratitude is pleasing to God and brings great blessing to our own hearts. When we add some of the hymns and choruses in our prayer time it brings added joy, comfort, courage, and yes, deep peace.

Many of the great songs of faith were forged out of extremely difficult circumstances. The words of these great songs can bring renewed strength to bring us through a valley.

As the nation of Israel was finally preparing to enter the Promised Land after forty years of wandering in the desert, God instructed Moses and Joshua (Deuteronomy 31 & 32) about a special heart preparation that was necessary before they could cross over.

You see, everyone who had been rescued from slavery in Egypt and had witnessed the miraculous Red Sea deliverance was gone. They had all died during the wilderness trek. Only Caleb and Joshua remained of that huge host who had started out on the journey, so God told the leaders that He wanted all of Israel to come together for a special time of remembering and worship.

He told them that they all needed to sing the "Song of Moses" again. It was the same song they had sung when they were rejoicing with the victory they had experienced at the parting of the Red Sea.

Why was such a preparation necessary? Because the Song of Moses is a song of courage, it's a reminder to be strong. It reminded them to be thankful. It's a reminder that God could meet their needs. The song recalled in their minds that God loves and cares for His children. It says that He hovers over His people like an eagle hovers over its young. Those were all truths God wanted His people to recall vividly and often.

The truth is, we are changed by who or what we choose

to worship. We become like the object of our worship. No wonder we are reminded to look to God in worship, and in all things to give thanks. He knows it's one of our deepest needs. It puts our lives into perspective.

Some years ago, a young mother found herself in an untenable situation. The man she loved, and loved to be with had become a different person. During the week everything moved along quite normally, but on weekends, when he drank heavily, he became violent, often beating her and their two children. She was frantic, and not knowing where to turn she decided to take the children and run to the little church just a couple of blocks away. It became a routine practice nearly every weekend.

Finally, she found enough courage to open her heart to the kind pastor who listened to her plight. He gave her a church key with the invitation, "Please come here whenever you are afraid. There will be blankets and pillows here and some food for you and the children. We want you to stay here as long as you need to. You'll be safe here."

So this became the practice. The mother and her children looked forward to going to the church. There they had peace, security, quiet, rest, stories, songs, and there they felt surrounded by love.

Eight-year old Michael remembers many nights sleeping on a church pew under a borrowed blanket, and enjoying warm food that kind church members had left for them.

Choosing to focus on these experiences rather than on the pain of his childhood, he and his family chose to live with gratitude. He looked to the pastor as a role model, and later Michael himself would become a pastor.

Gratitude for the love and care they had received, even in the midst of their pain, changed their lives. It brought a new sense of purpose and a new direction. And it built warm memories in the heart of an eight-year old who learned that God could always be trusted.

Life being what it is, this one thing I know about you: You are either in a storm, just coming out of a storm, or there is one just ahead. One of the essential steps for coming through that storm strong is to trust your life in the hand of God and choose to live a life of gratitude. Try it; you'll see.

It is often difficult
to see reasons to be grateful
when the wind is still blowing.

chapter 3

The Best Way Back to the Sunlight

"Give the world the best you have and the best will come back to you."

—Madeline Bridges

God puts us here on this planet to impact one another in some way.

Someone said, "Friends are angels who lift us to our feet when our wings have trouble remembering how to fly."

Recent studies show that 50% of those who experience a life of giving, have what is often called, "helpers' high." They have discovered that a life of service to others pays huge rewards.

My husband and I know a woman who has recently gone through a painful divorce. Even though she was experiencing some professional success, she was devastated. Her comment about that period in her life was that she didn't really know the meaning of peace until she chose to spend her time and energies in helping others. She made this powerful observation: "A great pain can only be fixed with a great purpose." She has been involved in raising funds for schools and children's homes in undeveloped countries, and it has changed her life.

She now would tell you that, "Givers are the real receivers." Giving has its own inherent reward. If you want to receive, start giving. This is the exciting way to live. It not only brings peace, but great fulfillment.

John Bunyan, who wrote the great classic, Pilgrim's Progress, said, "You haven't really lived today until you have done something for someone who cannot pay you back."

The amazing thing is that when we unselfishly reach out to bless someone, we help ourselves even more. It changes us, softens our hearts, and makes us happy and productive. It changes our whole outlook.

Recently we became acquainted with a lovely lady who lives on the west coast of the United States and she told us this story...we'll call her Irene.

Irene was devastated when her husband of 46 years died after only a brief illness and she found herself a widow. When the funeral was over and her family began returning to their own homes, Irene felt herself beginning to slide into a dark chasm. She didn't want to see anyone, didn't have her usual joy, and seldom ventured outside her small home.

Early one morning she awoke to another of her bleak, predictable days, but she began to sense what was happening to her. She decided she wanted no part of it—that her husband would not have wanted her just to hibernate; she had too much to give.

That morning Irene began to pray that God would somehow help her to see through different eyes, to make new friends, and to be able to *help someone*. She wasn't sure what to do or even where to start. Each day was like the one before, doing her routine chores but lacking the energy she had once known.

"Lord," she prayed, "I'm so lonely, but I believe You still have a purpose for my life; I just don't know how to go on alone. Please help me."

About that time, her friend and prayer partner, Janet, gave her a book.* It was filled with stories of fascinating but simple ways to reach out to others with some encouragement. She realized that the more she thought about herself, the worse she felt, and she seriously wanted to enlarge her horizon.

So she read the book, then read it again. And again. It spoke to her, and it seemed to say, "Irene, you can do this. You can make friends. You can make a difference in the lives of others."

"But how? How about some specifics, Lord."

During breakfast the next morning, she realized that she loved to bake. And she was known among her friends as a really good cook. "So, maybe I can turn that skill into a ministry to reach other lonely, needy people in my neighborhood," she pondered.

The first person she visited was a close neighbor who had acute leukemia and was in the throes of chemotherapy. She

*The book was, "Bridges 101, gas pumps, banana bread, and other attitudes," available at Amazon.com or at www.Bridges101.com.

was weak, depressed, and unable to fix balanced meals for herself.

Irene began to take food to her every morning and it wasn't long before she could watch her neighbor's mood changing right before her eyes. And it was more than the strength her body was receiving from the nourishing food, the neighbor's *heart* was also encouraged by this new friend who brought her food every day for weeks.

Irene soon found others she could help, so her kitchen became a center for ministry. Her neighbors looked forward to her visits—not just for the food, but for her smiles and words of encouragement. Today Irene has a big "route" she visits regularly. These folks have become her special people. She has bonded with them and they have become good friends.

But she didn't stop there. She got so excited about the changes she was seeing in her own life that she called her son who teaches in a university in Tennessee and told him about the book. He bought copies for some of his colleagues at the university; it was placed in the library, and it became required reading for the students in one of his classes.

His students said that as they practiced these simple but effective principles of "helping someone else" they discovered it helped *them* even more. We spoke to some of the students and one girl told us, "I feel like I'm a better person. I look at people differently." Another student said, "I work in the university library, and I'm very shy, but because of the book and the class assignment, I've started to make it a practice to make eye contact with people as they come into the library, and I smile. Now that may not seem like anything to some people, but for me it's a *big deal* and it really makes me feel good."

The students did simple things…leaving quarters for the washers and dryers at the Laundromat in town, looking for students who needed help with something…not rocket science, just thoughtfulness, just kindness.

Mother Teresa said it well, "We cannot do great things; only little things with great love."

Irene will tell you today, "These adventures have changed me! I'm a different person, and I love it."

Jesus never instructed His people to do the difficult. He didn't say, "I was sick and you built me a hospital. I was in prison and you helped to liberate me." No, He just says, "You visited Me, you clothed Me, you gave Me food; even a cup of cold water is noticed as something great in the eyes of heaven when it fills a need for someone."

Maybe you heard the amazing story about twin girls, Kyrie and Brielle, who were born in Worcester Memorial Hospital in Massachusetts. Though the babies were premature and weighed only two pounds at birth, Kyrie seemed to do well. But Brielle had trouble breathing and cried a great deal.

It soon became evident that Brielle was struggling for her life. The medical team did all they knew to do but she was no better, only worse. Then Gayle Kasparian, a nurse in the hospital's Neo-natal Intensive Care Unit, suggested a bold plan. She asked if she could go against hospital protocol and put the babies together in the same incubator, rather than in separate incubators. It was a big ordeal but finally the doctor and hospital agreed to allow the twins to be placed side by side in the same incubator, just as they had been in their mother's womb.

Somehow Kyrie managed to reach over and put her arm around her little sick sister. Before long, and for no apparent reason, Brielle's heart began to stabilize and heal. Her blood pressure normalized, and her temperature soon followed suit. Little by little she got better and today they are both healthy children.

The *Worcester Telegram and Gazette* heard about the incident, and a reporter, Chris Christo, was sent to photograph the twins while they were still in the incubator, embraced in a hug. The photo with the caption, "The Rescuing Hug," ran in *Life* magazine and the *Readers' Digest*.

God is seeking to enter the heart of every person on this planet—with hope. And the wonderful message of the Gospel must be spoken and shown to a watching world. You were made to be a giver. Who needs to feel your life-giving touch today? We serve God best and are never closer to Him than when we are serving others.

He asks us to do simple, loving deeds for His glory. If we are praying for others and asking that God will bless our efforts, He can and will use *anything* we are willing to do for Him in obedience to His call. No fanfare, no hoopla, no media coverage, just good people praying for others, and doing good things.

It is by the kindness of God that we are saved and when we pass this on God can do His wonders because He is "not willing that any should perish." He will lead you to prayerwalk,

35

The *best way* back to
the *sunlight* is often to *step out*
of our *comfort zone.*

or to share a loaf of bread or a plate of cookies. There may be someone in your neighborhood who needs your help right now.

Is there someone you could take to lunch? Is there someone who needs a lawn mowed? Does a young mother need some babysitting so she can do some shopping or just have a little quiet time?

When you are asking God for guidance, you will find Him leading you to someone He loves, someone who needs Him. Look around and ask Him who He wants you to bless today.

We are never closer to the heart of God than when we have reported for service. He often asks us to do simple things, like standing at the bedside of one of God's senior citizens, maybe not even talking—just being there. Or listening while a youngster practices his reading lesson. Or how about contacting someone you've been missing at church lately?

When you intentionally look at others through God's eyes He'll show you how He wants to love them through you.

So, here's the question: Are you feeling like you're 'stuck in a storm?' Do you know someone who is? When you look for someone who needs you, you probably won't have to look far. You'll find someone, maybe someone very near to you.

And the best way back to the sunlight is to step out of your comfort zone, and into the life of someone who needs just what you can give. That is when your life takes on new meaning, and you know that you are living the life He intended for you.

These are simple things, but our Father calls this *real*

business. Kingdom business. And what could be more enno-bling than to know that we are co-workers with the God who put the stars in place?

Those of us who did not live through the anguish of World War II can probably never understand its horror. War is often described as akin to hell. World War II was nothing less.

War is also a school. A school with teachers and pupils and lessons. War also exposes cowards and creates heroes. It causes men and women to do what they did not think they could do, and to endure the unthinkable.

We don't read far into the history of World War II in Europe before we come across the term, the French Underground, sometimes called the French Resistance. These were the intrepid citizens of France on whose precious soil much of the war was waged. In spite of hardships beyond description they determined to create a loyal stealth force that would help defeat the Nazis.

Men, women, children, seemingly going about the daily business of living were often actually part of the quiet Resistance Movement. A farmer with a cartload of apples may have a wounded solider hidden beneath them as he made his eager way to medical care.

A young girl, skipping along the street toward school, may actually have a pistol concealed in the bottom of her lunch box.

One of the roles played by the French Underground was to watch for Allied airmen who were shot down during bombing raids on Nazi fortifications. The loyal French would search for the men, often wounded, nurse them back to health and then smuggle them out of the country back to freedom.

To smuggle a soldier out of France and back to friendly territory was not an assignment for the fainthearted. To be caught meant certain death to the Allied airmen and to the would-be smugglers as well. Travel had to be done at night, on foot, with the group hiding in fields or abandoned buildings during daylight.

And there were the mountains... If you have traveled in France you know that it is a luxuriant country bounded by some of the most beautiful mountains in the world...mountains that do not lend themselves comfortably to foot traffic, at night, with the wounded.

So draw this picture in your mind: Five Allied airmen, recently wounded, with a single French Underground member as guide. Under cover of darkness they make their painful way cross-country and into the Alps. By day they hide, in the heat or cold, from those who would do them harm.

The mountains were the hardest. The climb is taxing to the best athletes, the best nourished, and the best equipped. These men were none of those. A single misstep in the darkness could mean further injury or a fatal fall. And the fatigue was at a level none of them had known before. Malnourished. Primitive health care. The outcome anything but certain.

Not all made it; amazingly, many did.

The French Underground made enough of these rescue sorties that they had learned a key truth. Let me describe it.

One of the jobs of the French guide was not only to find

the right path, but to keep the men moving and motivated. They had learned that if someone gave up, it was likely the end of the trail for him. Further, if a straggler was discovered it often revealed that others trying to escape were nearby and the Gestapo would launch a search-and-destroy mission for the escapees.

So, if a soldier stopped or fell, the others goaded him on. If he stopped again, they picked him up and pushed him in the direction of the top. If he fell again, they were relentless in urging him to keep on. Finally, a soldier, not fully recovered from the crash of his aircraft, debilitated and hungry, fatigued beyond description, would slump to the ground and collapse. No amount of pleading would motivate him to go on. So the guides developed a strategy.

They would give the struggling soldier a few minutes to rest, then they would turn aggressive and give him this ulti-matum: You can give up if you wish, but you are obligated to help the rest of us get to freedom. So you are to give your last measure of strength to the common good. We have a man here who is wounded as badly as you are, and who probably won't make it without some help. You are to put his arm around your shoulder and help him toward the top till you can't go another step. Then you are to go another step. And another. When you cannot move another inch you can quit, but not before you have poured your last measure of strength into saving a comrade.

Racked by pain and fatigue the soldier would stand to his feet and pour his last ounce of strength into helping his buddy.

And the fascinating part of the story is this: More often than not, *both* of them made it to freedom.

There is a new strength that seeps into our souls when, in our own time of distress, we do something noble to help someone else.

A great pain
can only be fixed
with a great purpose.

Chapter 4

What's Going On Around Here?

"Every thought is a seed.
If you plant crab apples,
don't count on harvesting
golden delicious."

—Bill Meyer

Your thoughts are powerful because they influence everything you do.

Your thoughts can make you gloomy or happy, lazy or productive, moral or immoral, gentle or rude, irate or calm, brash or shy, generous or miserly.

Then here's an important question: Where do our thoughts come from?

Well, that's a tricky question, and the answer is beyond the scope of this book. But here is a truth we can count on: Our thoughts are influenced by every sound we hear, every song we hear (or sing), every word we hear (or say), every sight we see, every experience we have, every influence that touches us.

Wow. That doesn't leave out much.

And here's a biggee: *What you <u>think</u> is who you are.*

Pardon?

Years ago I read a statement by Earl Nightingale which said, "You become like what you think about."

The wisest man who ever lived, King Solomon, said it best, "As [a person] thinks in his heart, so is he." (Prov 23:7)

If it's true then that we are what we think, and if it's true then that everything we do, see, hear, and experience influences our thoughts, then it follows that negative people, the wrong kind of television, movies, reading material, video games, the internet, all affect our lives at deep levels.

Let me be specific…

Remember when the talk around the water cooler was about I Love Lucy, and Andy of Mayberry? Or Bill Cosby and Bob Newhart? Have you been amazed as I have to watch the move away from simple sitcoms and programs with ennobling themes toward the questionable? Then way past the questionable to the lewd, vile, violent, dark, the depraved…

The problem is that if we're not careful we can begin to look at deviant behavior as normal, as acceptable, as ok.

How did that happen? How did we get from there to here?

Maybe Alexander Pope was on to something when he wrote:

> *Vice is a monster of so frightful mien,*
> *As to be hated need but to be seen;*
> *Yet seen too oft, familiar with her face,*
> *We first endure, then pity, then embrace.*

In 21st century parlance that means, even the most wretched of influences can become acceptable if we keep watching them. And every time we watch them they change who we are.

Now I'm not picking on country music, but I once heard it said you can be sure that with every country music song somebody is going to lose his girlfriend, his dog, or his pickup. If that's true then a fair question might be, Does it affect my thoughts if my mind is constantly rehearsing the stories of losers?

In March of this year my husband and I were at home eating lunch watching a news report on the Fox News channel. Fox reported that an eight-year study had just concluded that "Optimistic people were less apt to die of heart disease and cancer than their pessimistic peers." It went on to tell of research done by Dr. Leigh Vinocur of the University of Maryland School of Medicine that discovered, "…when people listen to music that makes them happy—that they think is joyful—it dilates their blood vessels." The report concluded that on the cellular level there is actually a release of hormones that can be beneficial.

Thus the question at the top of this chapter: "What's going on around here?" What's going on in your life? What are the influences that are shaping your thoughts that are shaping who you are? Are they helping you through the storm or keeping you stalled in it?

So here's an urgent issue to ponder: If I am constantly filling my mind with the same stuff that saturates our culture, are my thoughts going to be any different from all the others around me? Do I want my mind to be filled with the same decadent influences that so many others are feeding on?

Since you and I would probably agree that we want to make sure the answer to the last question is No, here is another question:

Who are your gatekeepers?

What's a gatekeeper? Let me explain...

About seven hundred years before the time of Christ, the great nation of China began construction on what would become one of the true architectural wonders of the world. In order to keep out her enemies, the people of China built a wall 25 - 30 feet high and 15 - 20 feet wide that would eventually stretch for more than 5,500 miles—from the eastern end of the empire to the west. That's further than the distance from New York City to San Francisco and all the way back to Atlanta. Some fence.

Most of the wall was actually completed during the Ming Dynasty (1368 - 1644) and an estimated 3,000 miles of the wall still stands. My husband visited there a while ago and brought back some spectacular photographs. It is truly an ancient wonder.

Since the building of the wall stretched over several centuries, it is difficult to know how many workers were part of the construction. Most of the work was done by Chinese soldiers, farmers, and prisoners. Some estimates place the number of workers who died during construction at more than 2,000,000. At its peak the wall was guarded by more than a million soldiers.

Your *thoughts* are *powerful* because they influence *everything* you do.

So, how well did it work in keeping out China's enemies?

It depends. No nation was ever successful in amassing an army sufficient to breach the wall and attack the country. Then it worked as a successful deterrent?

Not quite. At regular intervals along the wall the Chinese engineers had designed towers with doorways at ground level so the soldiers could do repair and maintenance on both sides. On those occasions when China's enemies were able to gain access to the nation and attack her, they usually gained access through the walls *simply by bribing the guards*.

So the elaborate, expensive, extraordinary efforts to provide protection to a nation were all compromised by the smallest of details.

So, back to my question: Who are *your* gatekeepers?

Since we have decided that every influence touching our lives affects how we think—which affects who we are, how do we keep out the bad stuff? Who are our personal gatekeepers?

Our choices.

Let me say some more about that. Every day we make choices about which influences we are going to permit to touch us. Good friends, positive and kind people, wrong friends, negative people...all have a slow, but life-changing impact. Entertainment that debases rather than ennobling. Wrong influences in our lives can be chipping away at the moral fiber on the inside almost without our notice until one day we discover we're in the middle of a major storm and don't have the spiritual resources to get through it.

I heard about a man who had a large boulder on his property

46

he wanted to break so he could move it. Each day with his hammer and chisel he went out for an hour, sometimes two, and took hard, direct swings at the rock, pounding away. But nothing happened. He doggedly kept at his task. Every day, he swung as hard and as long as he could. Always with the same result—nothing. He was tempted to think he was just wasting his time, but then one day, after weeks of pounding, the huge rock split in two.

Unbeknown to him, with each blow the integrity of the rock was slowly being compromised on the inside, until one day, it finally split wide open.

That is why every decision is important. Watch this carefully: Scripture tells us that each of us has two natures within— a carnal nature and a spiritual nature. Our carnal nature is the one we're born with, and it disobeys and rebels as readily as water runs down hill. Our spiritual nature is the one we are given when we surrender to God's loving invitation and He begins to change us on the inside.

Here's the issue: whichever nature we feed—the carnal or the spiritual—is the one that will grow stronger. And the one that is stronger ultimately determines what we become. That's why it is true: Every choice changes us.

That's no doubt what inspired the Apostle Paul to write, "Finally… whatever is true, whatever is noble, whatever is right, whatever is pure, whatever is lovely, whatever is admirable— if anything is excellent or praiseworthy—think about such things." (Phil 4:8)

Megyn Kelly, an anchor on FOX News, was asked why she "did a little dance" at the close of some of her newscasts.

She was actually seated so her "dance" wasn't what you might expect. She replied by saying that sometimes the news was so depressing she couldn't stand it, so she would ask the engineers to play some upbeat music, and even though she was seated, she moved back and forth on her stool in time to the happy rhythms. She saw how the news was affecting her and her viewers, and felt that she had to do something to try and leave everyone in a more pleasant frame of mine. She gets it.

So we're back to the subject of gatekeepers—*our choices.*

I have no desire to build a list of things I think you should or shouldn't watch or hear or do. To-do lists and to-don't lists usually aren't good vehicles for growth anyway. But here is what I would like to do. As one of the secrets for finding peace in a storm, I'd like to urge you to weigh carefully the kinds of influences that are bombarding your mind and heart daily.

Be willing to ask honestly, "What's going on around here…?" about those influences that are helping to make you what you are. Include your music, your entertainment, your friends, your reading, your hobbies, your thought life. You'll find this recommendation is a *huge secret* to finding peace in a storm.

Even the most wretched of
influences can become acceptable
if we keep watching them.

Chapter 5

God Really Likes You

God is pictured only once in the Bible as running... in the Prodigal Son story the father runs, arms outstretched, toward someone who was totally undeserving.

A aron, a young man who had joined a motorcycle gang, soon found his life going from bad to worse. He had the "uniform" of his gang, long hair, shaggy beard, tattoos, drugs, alcohol, guns. He was in and out of jail. He was known as a mean dude, and lived a life of crime. He would later say that he knew his life was completely out of control.

Every morning, to deaden the pain in his life, the first thing Aaron did was to get either drunk or high. One day as he looked into the mirror he seemed to see a "dead man" staring back at him. But he had a mother who never gave up on him, and a God who wouldn't give up either.

One Mother's Day, Aaron found his way into a church and

was ushered all the way up front to the second row. He wasn't quite sober, but somehow the message of the sermon reached his heart and though his brain was foggy, God spoke to him that morning. After the service he went outside, knelt down beside his motorcycle, and there in the parking lot gave his heart to Christ. He asked God to forgive his sins and to make him new.

You'll rejoice to know that Aaron, the former gang member, is now a pastor and travels all over the world sharing the joy of knowing and serving a God of love. His mother's prayers were answered and she sees God's goodness every day in the changed life of her son. It's amazing how God takes someone who, from a human perspective, has wandered so far from Him, and uses that very one to be a "person of honor" for His glory.

The incredible truth is that when the enemy tells you that you're worthless and reminds you of your sins and failures, God is there to say, "I'll take you. You are mine. I'm crazy about you." During the tough times the enemy comes at us with his lies to try to get us off track. This is when it's essential to remember that *no one has ever lived that God loved any more than He loves you right now.*

In uncountable ways God speaks to us and wants us to hear His heart say, "I love you…I have your picture on My refrigerator!"

The beautiful truth is that when we sense we are weak, we can be strong in His strength. 2 Corinthians 12:10 assures us of that fact. That's an amazing promise, really, from a loving God who values you as someone special. Yes, *you*. God not only loves you, He really likes you.

It's excitedly encouraging to know that no matter what weaknesses we think we have, no matter what inadequacies or obstacles or problems we've encountered, God wants to give us His divine strength. He makes up the difference in our brokenness and makes us whole. God loves to surprise us by the way He turns things around in our lives.

One Friday night my husband and I were driving in the beautiful state of Oregon and listening to sacred music on the car radio. We heard a little song neither of us had ever heard before, simple but profound in its message:

> *You're special to Jesus, His love you can't deny,*
> *You're special to Jesus, you're the apple of His eye.*
> *No matter what you're going through,*
> *no matter where you've been,*
> *You'll always be, special to Him.*

Great message of hope! We've sung it in places where we've spoken all over the world, and I've had people call me to ask for the words and melody of that little song...if I would sing it for them over the telephone. It had meant something to them, and they wanted to remember it and be blessed by it again. You might want to read it again right now, and where the song says, "you," insert the word, "I."

All through the Scripture record we see God at work. Sometimes He chooses to work almost secretively, sometimes He steps in suddenly. But He loves to come to us in our times of distress and whisper, "Remember, I'm still here; you can trust Me." And He does His miraculous work in our lives, not just because He *can*, but because He is *faithful*.

I know, sometimes we feel that we've made such a mess of things that we are not worthy of His care. Let me tell you about Brandon...

One Sunday morning six year-old Brandon decided to fix breakfast for his mom and dad. He found a big bowl and spoon, pulled a chair to the counter and opened the cupboard. The flour canister was heavier than he gauged it would be, and when he pulled it out, it slipped out of his hands and landed upside down on the floor. The lid rolled across the kitchen and banged into the refrigerator.

He scooped up some of the flour with his hands and mixed in most of a cup of milk, then added some sugar, leaving a floury trail on the floor—which by now had a few tracks left in it by his kitten, Eloise. Brandon was covered with flour by this time and was getting increasingly disgusted. He wanted this to be something nice for Mom and Dad, but it was not heading in that direction.

He didn't know what to do next, whether to put it all into the oven or on the stove, and he didn't know how either of them worked anyway.

Brandon looked up to see Eloise licking from the pancake bowl and as he reached to push her away, he knocked the egg carton off the counter. "I'd better get this cleaned up," he thought to himself, but the more he tried to clean up the monumental mess the more of it he got on himself.

Just then Brandon saw something that struck fear to his

heart…Dad was standing at the door. Big tears welled up in Brandon's eyes. All he had wanted to do was make a nice surprise for mom and dad, but instead he'd made a terrible mess. He was sure a scolding was coming, maybe worse. But his father just watched, then began to smile.

Tiptoeing through the mess, he picked up his crying son and squeezed him hard, not even minding the sticky mess now on his own pajamas. Mom appeared and soon the kitchen was back to its original shine and all three were sitting around the table eating her delicious pancakes.

That's how God deals with us. We set out to accomplish something and it turns into a mess. Sometimes we just stand there in tears because we can't think of anything else to do. That's when God picks us up and loves us and forgives us, even though some of our mess gets all over Him.

You are loved and valued by God. He has a wonderful plan and purpose for your life. His Word says that He thinks good thoughts about you. He promises to make you strong as you get to know Him intimately.

His Word tells us that He is a God of abundance. Abundant blessings. Abundant gifts. Abundant mercy. He wants to pour out His abundance on us until we are so full that we are running over with His joy and are equipped for any storm.

Eric discovered that same truth not long ago. Eric was a felon, rightfully convicted under the laws of his state. However, as he was serving his time in the state penitentiary he came in contact with some Christians who helped him see that even though he had made some terribly bad choices,

God still loved him with an unconditional love.

When Eric's friends introduced him to Scripture he began to read it like a man thirsting to know what God would tell him next.

And his life began to change. When he finally served his time for the crime he had committed, Eric came out of prison a changed man. He was able to finish his college degree and then go to work for a small company where he could use his skills. His supervisors in the company were soon aware of the integrity and abilities of their new employee and they also watched his ability to encourage and inspire others. They were surprised at the promise he showed and kept promoting him as far as they could.

One day the president of the company called Eric into his office and invited him to sit down. "Eric," he began, "I'm sorry to have to tell you this because I think you'd make a very good vice-president in this company, but we cannot give you that position

Rest secure in the knowledge that He loves you.

because of your past record. As a convicted felon, even though you served your sentence and your life is totally changed, our board feels that it might expose us to legal difficulty down the road and they are not willing to take that chance. You deserve the job, and I wish I could offer it to you, but I can't."

Eric prayed for wisdom. He seemed to sense that maybe God had bigger plans for him. So after much thought and prayer and after discussing the matter with his pastor, he contacted the Board of Pardons for his state and asked for an appointment. Finally the day arrived. It was not easy to sit there in the large court room hour after hour and listen to the pleas of others who were also there to request pardons.

When it came Eric's turn he went forward and stood quietly.
When he was asked why he thought he should be pardoned he replied simply, "Sir, I don't deserve a pardon. I am a felon. I committed a terrible crime, and although I paid for it with a

prison sentence I really don't deserve to be pardoned. I have become a Christian, and I will accept whatever you think is best for me."

It took weeks for all of the records to be evaluated. Then one day he received an official looking notice in the mail from the Board of Pardons.

After a couple of paragraphs of legal mumbo-jumbo, Eric read this astonishing sentence and the words swam before his eyes: "After careful review of all of the information at hand, *the Board of Pardons has granted you a full pardon.*"

It took Eric a few minutes to realize the significance of their words. The implications were staggering. Today if you were to look for the records of Eric's crime in the records of the state of Nebraska there would be *nothing* in his file. It's gone. There is nothing there. A full pardon means there is no record of the crime and no trace of the sentence.

And that's our story, too. Your story and mine.

There's a wonderful old gospel song that says it so well:

Tis so sweet to trust in Jesus, just to take Him at His Word.
Just to rest upon His promise, just to know thus saith the Lord.
Jesus, Jesus, how I trust Him, how I've proved Him o'er and o'er.
Jesus, Jesus, precious Jesus, O for grace to trust Him more.

Thank Him every day for the privilege of trusting Him, and for the privilege of taking Him at His Word. Rest secure in the knowledge that He loves you. He has taken care of your past, provides strength for your present, and has made full provision for your future. Man, what a God!

You may remember the thrilling stories written about World War II by Corrie ten Boom, the Dutch writer and speaker. I had the great privilege of talking to her numerous times by phone before she died, and I will never forget the courage that came to me each time we spoke. I heard a wonderful story about her, about how she would sometimes hold her Bible up in the air as she prayed. She would open it to a specific promise, point to it, and then she would pray, "Lort," (that's Dutch for Lord), "Lort, here is your promise. Read it for yourself. You must do something, and there is no time to waste."

Through Corrie's experiences in a German prison camp during the war she came to know God intimately, and learned that she could trust Him. God must have enjoyed His conversations with her because she saw Him provide for her needs time after time.

He loves and values you too. You have His word that He will never leave you or forsake you. His plans and purposes for you are *good*. Your best days are just ahead. He has promised. You can trust Him. And just think—one day you can thank Him in person!

He loves to come to us in our
times of distress and whisper,
"Remember, I'm still here; you can trust Me."

5 secrets

Summing up

1

Watch your words – both your own
and of those around you.

2

Consistently focus on what you've got,
not what you've lost.

3

Be resourceful and persistent about
finding ways to help others.

4

Take care that only healthy, positive
influences are allowed into your mind.

5

Always remember that you are one
of God's very special friends.

'Til The Storm Passes By

In the dark of the midnight have I oft hid my face,
While the storm howls above me, and there's no hiding place.
'Mid the crash of the thunder, precious Lord, hear my cry,
Keep me safe till the storm passes by.

Chorus
Till the storm passes over, till the thunder sounds no more,
Till the clouds roll forever from the sky,
Hold me fast, let me stand in the hollow of Thy hand,
Keep me safe till the storm passes by.

Many times Satan whispered, "There is no need to try,
For there's no end of sorrow, there's no hope by and by."
But I know Thou art with me, and tomorrow I'll rise
Where the storms never darken the skies.

Chorus
Till the storm passes over, till the thunder sounds no more,
Till the clouds roll forever from the sky,
Hold me fast, let me stand in the hollow of Thy hand,
Keep me safe till the storm passes by.

Lyrics & music by Mosie Lister

Our way of saying thanks...

A̲s our thank you for purchasing this book we would like to give you a free download of what may be one of the most magnificent and encouraging songs you have heard in a long time.

Go to the website below, put in the User ID and Password, and at no cost you are invited to download the mp3 of, "Til the Storm Passes By," a wonderful song written by Mosie Lister, and sung by one of my all time favorite music groups, Greater Vision. My friend, Gerald Wolfe, lead of the group, does the solo; the majestic accompaniment is performed by the Prague Symphony Orchestra.

The song is really a prayer so listen with your heart as well as your ears. It will be a glorious conclusion to the words you have just read in the book and it is our gift to you. I promise that you are going to love this music.

Website: **www.RuthieJacobsen.com/bonus**
User ID: **music**
Password: **091634-1102**

Gerald Wolfe,
manager and lead
Greater Vision trio